BEAUTIFUL LAND

Everyone was waiting for the signal to cross over into the Oklahoma Territory and stake a claim.

Annie Mae was restless. It seemed years since they had listened to the preacher speak. He had talked about the blessings they were about to receive. He also said, "I know there will be fights about land." He warned the settlers against using guns. "Settle your fights in the land office," he said.

The preacher had meant to be comforting. But his words only gave Annie Mae more things to worry about. Would someone really shoot at them if they wanted the claim Pa staked?

It seemed as if it would never be noon. Annie Mae was so excited—and worried.

Slowly the sun climbed higher in the sky. Then it was almost directly overhead. Annie Mae noticed that everything around her had gotten very quiet.

As Annie Mae watched, a soldier rode forward. He put a shiny bugle to his lips. For a single instant, she heard the call of its horn. Then it was drowned out by a thunderous roar. Horses' hooves clattered, wagons clanked and strained. And everywhere people hollered and shouted for joy.

Pa slapped the horses hard. Their wagon crossed over into Oklahoma.

Beautiful Land

Beautiful Land

A STORY OF THE OKLAHOMA LAND RUSH

BY NANCY ANTLE

ILLUSTRATED BY JOHN GAMPERT

PUFFIN BOOKS

To Rick, my best friend and,

happily, my husband

PUFFIN BOOKS
Published by the Penguin Group
Penguin Books USA Inc., 375 Hudson Street, New York, New York 10014, U.S.A.
Penguin Books Ltd, 27 Wrights Lane, London W8 5TZ, England
Penguin Books Australia Ltd, Ringwood, Victoria, Australia
Penguin Books Canada Ltd, 10 Alcorn Avenue, Toronto, Ontario, Canada M4V 3B2
Penguin Books (N.Z.) Ltd, 182-190 Wairau Road, Auckland 10, New Zealand

Penguin Books Ltd, Registered Offices: Harmondsworth, Middlesex, England

First published in the United States of America by Viking,
a division of Penguin Books USA Inc., 1994
Published in Puffin Books, 1997

3 5 7 9 10 8 6 4 2

THE LIBRARY OF CONGRESS HAS CATALOGED THE VIKING EDITION AS FOLLOWS:
Antle, Nancy.
Beautiful land : a story of the Oklahoma Land Rush / by Nancy Antle ;
illustrated by John Gampert.
p. cm.—(Once upon America)
Summary: After a two-year wait during which her mother died, twelve-year-old
Annie Mae and her family join thousands of hopeful settlers as they race
to claim land in the newly-opened Oklahoma Territory.
ISBN 0-670-85304-6
1. Oklahoma—History—Land Rush, 1889—Juvenile fiction.
[1. Oklahoma—History—Land Rush, 1889—Fiction.
2. Frontier and pioneer life—Oklahoma—Fiction.]
I. Gampert, John, ill.
II. Title. III. Series.
PZ7.A6294Be 1994 [Fic]—dc20 93-41482 CIP AC

Puffin Books ISBN 0-14-036808-6

Printed in the United States of America

ONCE UPON AMERICA® is a registered trademark of Viking Penguin,
a division of Penguin Books USA Inc.

Thanks to Dr. Stan Hoig, author of
The Oklahoma Land Rush of 1889, *for*
critiquing the first draft and answering my many questions,
and to Vicki Berger Erwin for her
constant encouragement and valuable criticism.

Contents

A New Life 1

Mud 9

Crossing the Salt Fork 16

Land Run! 25

Claim Jumpers 34

Filing the Claim 42

About This Book 52

A New Life

A cool spring breeze ruffled Annie Mae's red hair. She pulled up her quilt. Her little brother, Dan, snored next to her in the darkness. Annie Mae was used to the sound. He had snored every night since he was born seven years ago. The door to their dugout was open a crack. Annie Mae could see the first orange glow of sunrise.

"Whoa!" Pa's voice came from outside.

Dan stirred. "What's Pa doing?" he mumbled sleepily.

"Harnessing the horses," Annie Mae whispered.

"Oh." Dan turned over on his stomach. Soon he was snoring again

Annie Mae smiled. He was too sleepy to remember about their trip.

She breathed deeply. The room smelled damp and earthy from the recent rains. She remembered the first time she had seen the dugout. They had left Missouri to come to Kansas. Ma's brother, Uncle Michael, had written that the Oklahoma Territory across the border would be open to settlers any day. He made the dugout for them to live in "for a little while," until the territory opened. A little while had turned into two years.

The dugout always looked to Annie Mae like it be-

longed in one of the fairy tales Ma used to tell. It was
a house dug out of the side of a hill, with dirt walls and
floor—and sticks and sod for a roof.

Only half a mile away, Uncle Michael, Aunt Ellen,
and their daughter, Libby, lived in one just like it.
Libby and Annie Mae liked to pretend that they were
fairy princesses living in secret caves in the ground.
Their kingdom was the prairie that seemed to stretch
forever into the distance.

The dugout kept them warm and snug in winter.
And it kept them safe in summer during twister
weather. It had been a good home for two years. It was
better than the sharecropper's shack they'd lived in
when Pa farmed someone else's land.

Annie Mae would be sorry to leave the dugout. It was the last place they had all been together with Ma. But they had to go. She knew that. Going to Oklahoma was their chance at a better life. A life where Pa and Uncle Michael and Aunt Ellen could farm for themselves instead of for someone else. A life where they wouldn't have to carry suitcases at the hotel, or clean house for rich folks, or unload freight for the railroad, or any of the other jobs they'd been doing while they waited.

"When they open the Oklahoma Territory," Ma used to say, "Pa and Uncle Michael are going to get the two most beautiful pieces of land in Oklahoma."

Now finally the president had agreed to open the land. There was going to be a land run. Pa said it would be like a big race. People would start at the line in horses and wagons and on foot. They would all race to pick out plots of land to farm.

They were going to have their chance at a new life. Today they were going to travel to the Oklahoma line with the other settlers. But Ma wouldn't be there with them. She had taken sick and died before she even got to hear that the territory had been opened.

Annie Mae swallowed the lump in her throat. She was going to make sure that Pa and Uncle Michael got beautiful pieces of land, just for Ma. No matter what.

"Annie Mae! Dan!" Pa called from the door of the dugout, "time to get up. Uncle Michael and Aunt

Ellen will be here soon." The two families were going to travel to the territory together. They would get land side by side if they could.

Annie Mae was glad that they would travel together. Since Ma died, though, Uncle Michael treated Annie Mae differently. He hardly ever talked to her. And he never looked at her. Pa said it was because she was so much like Ma. It made Uncle Michael sad to look at Annie Mae.

Annie Mae thought that was a stupid reason not to look at someone. Especially since Uncle Michael looked just like Ma, too. Annie Mae liked to look at him and remember Ma.

She wished Uncle Michael would look at her and smile sometimes—Ma's smile. She missed the old Uncle Michael, the one who used to laugh and tease her all the time.

Annie Mae sat up in bed. Dan moaned and pulled the quilt over his head.

"Dan, get up," Annie Mae said. Dan didn't move. Pa always said that he could sleep through a tornado.

"Dan!" Annie Mae shouted. She shook him by the shoulder. "We're going to Oklahoma!"

Dan sat up instantly. He rubbed his eyes.

"Hooray!" He jumped out of bed. He stumbled as he struggled to pull on his pants over his nightshirt. Annie Mae laughed and helped him with his clothes.

"We are going to go get our land at last!" Dan said. "I can't wait, Annie Mae. We're going to get a wooden house! And have chickens and pigs and cows! I hope we have water nearby. I'm tired of carrying water from the river, aren't you, Annie Mae?"

Annie Mae laughed again. "We'd better hurry and quit talking," she said. "We don't want to be the last Boomer family to leave." Dan giggled.

All the people who had been waiting were called Boomers. They got that name because they had been so loud about asking for permission to go to Oklahoma. Some of them, like Uncle Michael and Aunt Ellen, had been waiting ten years. Libby had lived her whole life waiting to go to Oklahoma.

Annie Mae pulled on her faded cotton dress. Dan buttoned up the back. Then he braided her long red hair for her. He chattered on while Annie Mae pulled up his suspenders and handed him his socks.

"Wouldn't Ma be happy today? I wish she was here. Don't you? Do you think she's watching us from heaven?"

Annie Mae swallowed hard.

"I'm sure she is," she said.

"When will we get our land? What will we live in until we have a house?"

"We'll live in a tent, and we'll get our land soon. The land run is only four days from now." Then Annie

Mae repeated what they'd heard in town last month: "It will be at high noon on the day after Easter Sunday, April 22, 1889."

Annie Mae and Dan picked up a wooden box of food, carrying it between them, and ran outside. The two horses, Blue and Belle, were hitched to the wagon. The canvas cover was in place over the top. The sky was clear and held the promise of good weather. Thank goodness, the thunderstorms had finally moved on.

They made four more trips to the dugout to get crates. The crates held food, clothes, and their few dishes and pots. Pa came in to help take apart the bed and load it into the wagon. The last thing to be loaded was Ma's rocking chair.

The three of them walked back into the dugout to take one last look around.

"I wish we could take the stove," Dan said. "It's going to be might cold without it."

"Mr. Herman paid us well for it," Pa said. "And we sure did need the money. We'll get another as soon as we're able."

"Good morning!" Uncle Michael called from outside.

"Time to go!" Dan shouted. He grabbed Annie Mae and Pa by the hands and pulled them outside.

Annie Mae waved to her cousin Libby. Libby smiled

and waved back. Annie Mae felt a stab of disappointment when Uncle Michael smiled at Dan, but not at her. Then everyone began talking at once.

"Aunt Ellen, can I eat my meals with you on the trip?" Dan asked. "Pa doesn't cook so well.""

"I beg your pardon," Pa said. He chuckled.

"You all can," Aunt Ellen said.

"Can Annie Mae ride with us?" Libby asked.

"Me, too," Dan said.

"Doesn't anyone want to ride with me?" Pa asked.

"Let's just put the kids in one wagon and us in the other," Uncle Michael said. "Save us a lot of trouble."

"Can we? Can we?" Dan shouted.

"I was teasing, Danny boy," Uncle Michael said. "Let's all ride in our own wagons till we get through town."

"Good," Pa agreed.

Annie Mae and Dan climbed into the wagon seat. Pa climbed up beside them and picked up the reins.

"Let's get this Boomer wagon going!" Pa yelled.

Mud

Everywhere on the prairie, tents were set up. People were waiting to go to Oklahoma. Some of them had only been waiting there a few weeks. Many wagons were starting to head south through town.

As they got closer, the wagons began moving into a line—one behind the other. Some excited person tried to cut into the line of wagons between Uncle Michael and Pa.

"Hey!" Pa shouted.

The man stopped his horses. He smiled a sheepish grin at Pa. "Sorry," he said.

"It's okay," Pa said. "I'm excited myself."

"He sure was rude to try and cut in line," Annie Mae said.

"I hope he won't try anything like that again," Pa said. "We're all in this together. If we don't help each other out—none of us is going to make it."

They got closer to town and headed down Summit Street. The narrow street was covered in mud. Deep, dark, black mud. They couldn't go around. A tall hedge was on one side of the street and a wire fence on the other.

"Not many wagons have gone through," Uncle Michael called to Pa. "It might not be too bad yet."

"Do you think we'll make it?" Annie Mae asked.

"We have to," Pa said. "This is the only road that leads south."

It isn't fair, Annie Mae thought angrily. This was supposed to be the easy part of the trip. Later there would be no roads. It couldn't be any worse than this, though.

Uncle Michael looked as angry as she was. Ma always said that Annie Mae had Uncle Michael's hot temper. Pa used to laugh when she said that.

"Of course she got none of that from you!" he'd tease. Ma would only laugh in reply. She couldn't argue. Her temper was just as hot—especially if someone treated her family badly. The grocer in town had charged Dan too much for a piece of candy once. When Ma was done with him, he never tried that again.

"Ma sure would be mad about all this mud," Annie Mae said.

Pa smiled and nodded. Then he frowned and pressed his lips together. He slapped the horses with the reins again.

Slowly, slowly, Blue and Belle pulled the wagon through the mud. Every time they stopped for a moment, Annie Mae held her breath. She waited to see if they would go on.

Suddenly, there was a sucking noise and a bump. The horses strained and whinnied. But the wagon didn't move. Pa handed the reins to Annie Mae.

"I have to push," he said.

Annie Mae passed the reins to Dan.

"I'll help."

Pa didn't try to stop her as she jumped down from the wagon. Up ahead, Uncle Michael and Aunt Ellen were getting down to push their own wagon.

The mud was almost to Annie Mae's knees. She felt it ooze into her shoes. She and Pa put their backs against the end of the wagon and pushed with their legs. Dan "gee-upped" to the horses.

The wagon moved forward with a sudden lurch. Annie Mae and Pa fell with a *splat* into the muddy

street. They looked at each other and burst out laughing. They were covered in mud from head to toe.

"We must want to go to Oklahoma awfully bad," Annie Mae said.

"We sure must," Pa said.

They continued out of town. Every so often, the wagon got stuck. Pa and Annie Mae got out to push. Sometimes they had to shovel the muck from under the wheels. The sun was high over their heads by the time they reached the end of the street.

In back of them, other wagons were trying to make it down the street. Most of them were getting stuck, too. People yelled and cursed at their horses and at each other. Women, men, and children all got out to push. Soon it was hard to tell who was who.

Suddenly Dan called out, "Uncle Michael and Aunt Ellen need help."

Annie Mae and Pa slogged around to the wagon. While Pa and Uncle Michael and Aunt Ellen decided what to do, Annie Mae went to the front to see Libby.

"It isn't fair to wait all these years and then have this mud in our way!" Annie Mae said.

Libby laughed.

"You and Pa sure are alike," she said. "That's just what he said."

"Well, it's true," Annie Mae said.

"Don't get so mad," Libby said.

"Don't act so calm," Annie Mae replied. "This is serious."

Annie Mae stomped back through the mud to help the others. Libby was only ten, two years younger than Annie Mae. They were best friends most of the time, but sometimes Libby just rubbed Annie Mae the wrong way. Libby was taller than Annie Mae and tried to act older. She was always so calm about everything. It made Annie Mae mad.

Pa said Libby couldn't help it. That's just the way she was. But Annie Mae was sure that sometimes she acted grown-up just to bother her and Dan.

Uncle Michael and Pa were shoving boards under the wheels of the wagon. When they were done, they all pushed with their backs. Dan got down and helped, too.

"I knew we should have left some of this stuff behind," Uncle Michael said.

Pa leaned into the wagon harder.

"You'll be glad you have it once you're in Oklahoma," he said. "It's always nice to have familiar things around you."

"If any of us ever see Oklahoma," Aunt Ellen said.

"Of course we'll see Oklahoma!" Annie Mae and Uncle Michael said together. Annie Mae glanced quickly over at her uncle. He didn't look back, but he was smiling. "We aren't going to let a little mud stop us," he said.

The wagon moved forward. Uncle Michael laughed

his big booming laugh. Annie Mae laughed with re-
lief, too.

Finally the wagon was free of the mud. It rolled on
steadily until it was on drier ground.

"Now our wagon has settled in the mud," Dan said.

Uncle Michael and Aunt Ellen came back to help
them push their wagon.

"Surely, the worst is over," Pa said.

"Surely so," Annie Mae agreed. Her body ached all
over and she was soaked to the skin. They all climbed
back into their wagons.

At the Arkansas River bridge she leaned out to look
behind them. There seemed to be an endless stream of
wagons with white tops. Hundreds of them.

"How much land is there in Oklahoma Territory,
Pa?" she asked.

"Two million acres," Pa answered. "All divided up
into plots of 160 acres."

Annie Mae looked at all the wagons again. Was the
worst really over? Would two million acres be enough?
What if someone beat them to the two most beautiful
pieces of land in Oklahoma?

Crossing the Salt Fork

"Do they want us to cross over on that?" Annie Mae asked. A weak-looking bridge, recently built, spanned the river.

Pa didn't answer. He just shook his head. Dan sat with his eyes wide.

They were staring at the Salt Fork River, a tributary of the Arkansas River. The river had flooded its banks because of the rains. It was a churning mass of water, tree limbs, and mud. It lay between them and the Oklahoma Territory line. They had to cross it.

"Sometimes it seems like we weren't meant to go to Oklahoma," Pa said quietly.

"Of course we were," Annie Mae snapped. "Captain Hayes will figure out a way. He has to."

"His men built that bridge so we could cross," Pa said. "It's already falling apart. He'll have to think of something fast or we won't be at the line on April 22."

Uncle Michael strode back to their wagon. His face was red.

"I'm going to see if Captain Hayes has a plan."

"I'll come with you," Pa said. Annie Mae and Dan climbed down from the wagon, too. Pa didn't stop them or Libby from following. They made their way through the wagons and people. Dan and Libby stayed close behind Annie Mae. Dan stepped on her heels twice. Libby ran right into her when she stopped suddenly.

"There's Captain Hayes," Annie Mae whispered.

Captain Hayes was the commander of a troop in the Fifth Cavalry. He and his men had met up with the settlers at the Indian Territory. They had been ordered to go with the settlers to the Oklahoma line. He was there to help them. But he was also there to make sure no one went into Oklahoma ahead of time.

He was dressed in a dark blue uniform. He stood surrounded by other men in uniform and settlers dressed in ordinary clothes. His voice was strong and deep. It was easy to hear him, even from where Annie Mae stood.

"The bridge we built has been damaged by the flood water. It's unsafe," he told his men. "I want you all to tell the settlers to make camp. We will have to come up with a different plan."

"What about the railroad bridge?" a settler shouted.

In the distance, Annie Mae could see the railroad bridge that spanned the river. It was a giant rectangle, with huge beams in Xs all along its sides. It looked solid and strong—and safe.

"Yes. Let's use the railroad bridge," another said. Others agreed.

"I'm on my way now to the Ponca Agency to telegraph the railroad office," Captain Hayes replied. "We have to get permission before we can use their bridge."

"I say we use it, whether they give us permission or not," someone said.

"That's right. There are too many of us. They can't stop us."

"Someone already tried the bridge," Captain Hayes said. "His horse broke its leg when it slipped between the ties. If the bridge is to be used, we have to cover it with planks to prevent another accident. Lookouts will have to be posted, too, to stop the trains."

Then Annie Mae watched as Captain Hayes mounted his horse and rode away.

When Captain Hayes returned, it was decided. The settlers and soldiers would cover the bridge with wooden planks to make it safe for the horses. The horses would be led across, separate from their wagons. That way, if a horse got scared and bolted, it wouldn't dump its wagon into the river. Groups of men would haul the wagons over.

Pa and Uncle Michael worked all night helping to get the bridge ready. In the morning, they returned to hitch their horses to the wagons. Then they followed the line of wagons and settlers to wait for a turn to cross the bridge.

The train tracks ran along the top of a steep mound. Getting the wagons up onto the tracks that ran across the bridge was tricky. Getting them back down at the end was worse. It took all of the men's strength to keep the wagons from rolling away.

Finally, it was their turn. Pa drove Blue and Belle up to the start of the railroad bridge. He handed Belle's lead to Dan and Blue's to Annie Mae. Then he joined the men who would pull their wagon across.

Halfway across, Annie Mae could hear Aunt Ellen back at the start of the bridge, yelling at one of her own horses. It was a skittish mare that always gave her and Uncle Michael trouble.

"You may have to make that one swim," one of the soldiers said.

"I don't want to take a chance on losing one of my horses, if I can help it," Aunt Ellen replied.

Annie Mae and Dan easily led Blue and Belle over

the bridge. They stood at the bottom of the hill. They watched as, slowly, their wagon was pulled across. Uncle Michael had come around to help Pa and the six other men. Pa would help him later.

Aunt Ellen followed soon after. She was still having trouble with the mare. The horse danced sideways whenever a board under her hooves made a loud sound. Libby led the family's other horse a safe distance behind.

Suddenly, Aunt Ellen's mare bolted.

"Look out!" Annie Mae yelled.

Pa and Uncle Michael and the other men were still struggling to get the wagon off the bridge and down the steep slope from the tracks.

Annie Mae's cry and the sound of the mare lumbering across the bridge made them all look up. Two of the men holding on to the back of the wagon slipped on the loose earth in their hurry to get out of the way. They lost their hold on the wagon. It started rolling faster. Two other men slipped and fell. The wagon rolled even faster—then it hit a bump and turned right toward the river. Pa and Uncle Michael were still holding on.

Annie Mae ran toward the wagon. She slipped and slid on the soft earth.

"Stop!" she yelled. "Please stop it! Pa, don't let it go into the river! It's all our things. Ma's things. Uncle Michael, hold on!"

With a giant splash, the wagon's front wheels landed in the Salt Fork River. Then it stopped. The tongue of the wagon was stuck deep in the mud.

Pa and Uncle Michael and the rest of the men sat down on the ground trying to catch their breath. They stared at the wagon. Some shook their heads.

Pa started to chuckle. "That sure scared me," he said. "I thought my wagon was a goner."

"You should have seen the look on your face," Uncle Michael said.

"You should have seen the look on *yours!*" someone else said.

Pretty soon all the men, and even Dan, were laughing.

Annie Mae put her hands on her hips. She glared at everyone. It seemed to make them laugh even harder.

"It's not funny!" she said. "It's not funny and it isn't fair! We've had enough trouble! We almost lost all our things. All Ma's things. How will we ever get to Oklahoma in time now?" She was so angry she was about to cry.

Libby and Aunt Ellen were beside her now.

"I'm so sorry," Aunt Ellen said. She put a strong arm around Annie Mae's shoulder. "That horse is the spookiest horse we've ever had. I should have made her swim."

"It's not your fault, Ellen," Pa said.

"Don't worry," Libby said to Annie Mae. "You can

ride with us if you have to. You'll still get to Oklahoma. I'm not going without my best friend."

Annie Mae smiled a little. For once she didn't mind her cousin's calmness.

"Of course you'll get to Oklahoma," Aunt Ellen said.

"Don't worry, little lady," a soldier said. He had the mare by the reins, and he handed them to Aunt Ellen. "We'll get a rope around your wagon and pull it out in no time."

"Sure we will," a settler said. "You'll get to the line by Easter Sunday with the rest of us. That's a promise."

Uncle Michael walked over. He looked right at Annie Mae. She was so surprised, her mouth dropped open.

"When you get mad, you sure do remind me of your ma," he said.

"I'm glad you do," Libby said. "I miss Aunt Mary."

Annie Mae felt a knot swell in the back of her throat.

"We all miss her," Aunt Ellen said. She hugged Annie Mae close to her.

Uncle Michael coughed and looked at the ground. Then he walked off quickly.

"He doesn't like to look at me," Annie Mae said. "He doesn't like to remember Ma."

"That's not true," Aunt Ellen said softly.

Annie Mae wanted to believe that more than anything. Just as she wanted to believe more than

anything that they would get to the line by Easter
Sunday like the settler said. But every time she
thought the worst of the trip was over, something else
happened. It made her wonder what would happen
next.

Land Run!

"It's beautiful," Annie Mae said. She was sitting beside Dan and Pa in the wagon seat. They were looking across at the Oklahoma Territory. Everywhere there were great patches of green, and colorful spring flowers. Over all of it, the sky was a brilliant blue.

Today was the day. At last, it was April 22, 1889. Soldiers in navy-blue uniforms rode up and down the line of wagons and horses. Everyone was waiting for the signal to cross over into the Oklahoma Territory and stake a claim. There were old people, young people, families, single men and women—on horses, in wagons, and on foot.

Annie Mae was restless. She hummed a few bars of "Nearer My God to Thee," which they had sung only yesterday on Easter Sunday. It already seemed like years had gone by since they had listened to the preacher speak.

He had talked about the blessings they were about to receive. He also said, "I know there will be fights about land." He warned the settlers against using guns. "Settle your fights in the land office," he said.

The preacher had meant to be comforting. But his words only gave Annie Mae more things to worry

about. Would someone really shoot at them if they wanted the claim Pa staked?

It seemed as if it would never be noon. Annie Mae was so excited—and worried.

Slowly the sun climbed higher in the sky. Then it was almost directly overhead. Annie Mae noticed that everything around her had gotten very quiet. Only the sound of horses snorting and stomping or the sound of squeaky saddles broke the stillness.

As Annie Mae watched, a soldier rode forward. He put a shiny bugle to his lips. For a single instant, she heard the call of its horn. Then it was drowned out by a thunderous roar. Horses' hooves clattered, wagons

clanked and strained. And everywhere people hollered and shouted for joy.

Pa slapped the horses hard. Blue and Belle crossed over into Oklahoma. Annie Mae was so happy, she thought she would burst.

"Look!" Dan said, pointing. An old man had crossed over the line and staked the first claim he came to. He was already plowing his farm.

"We should have done that," Annie Mae said. She was still afraid that there wouldn't be enough land for everyone.

"No," Pa said. "Uncle Michael says the land is better further on. He saw it when he worked for the railroad."

"Go faster, Pa," Annie Mae said.

A little later, they passed a campsite that looked as though it had been there a long time. There was a ring of stones for a fire. Wood was stacked beside it.

"Moonlighters," Pa said.

"What does that mean?" Annie Mae asked.

"They crossed the line by the light of the moon—so they wouldn't get caught. They got their claims long before we even left."

"That's not fair," Annie Mae said.

"We should tell someone," Dan added.

"They'll get caught sooner or later," Pa said. "Right now, we've got to stake our own claim."

Pa let the horses slow to a walk. Uncle Michael did

the same beside them. There weren't so many wagons and people around now.

After a while, they came to the top of a small rise. In front of them was a clear, level piece of land. Just beyond it, dogwood and redbud trees were in bloom. Behind the trees, the land sloped into a little rocky valley. It looked exactly as Annie Mae had imagined—the most beautiful piece of land in Oklahoma.

"Oh, Pa," Annie Mae said. "Let's start our new life here. Ma would have loved this place."

Pa looked over at Dan. "What do you think?"

"Yes," Dan said. "Stop here."

"I think I see a stone corner marker over there," Uncle Michael called to them. "I'll try to get the next quarter section over, if I can." Surveyors had laid out the land in sections. Each section was divided into quarters with stone markers at each corner. The markers would tell someone what number the claim was. Pa said the hardest part about staking a claim was going to be finding the markers. And then making sure no one else was on your claim.

Pa jumped down just as another wagon came over the rise. He grabbed his stake with the white flag. Annie Mae and Dan got down to help him drive it into the ground.

Annie Mae held her breath as the wagon drove toward them. There was only one man in it. Would he pull out his gun and argue with Pa about the land?

"You got yourself a pretty nice place for a farm," the man said. "I sure wish I'd beaten you to it. Good luck anyway."

Pa smiled and nodded at the stranger. Annie Mae let out her breath. Maybe the preacher was wrong about people arguing over the claims.

"Annie Mae, you and Dan go see if you can spot Uncle Michael and Aunt Ellen. I hope they got that claim," Pa said. "I'll set up our tent. It will make it look like we're planning to stay awhile."

Annie Mae smiled at Pa, then gave him a quick hug. She and Dan ran off toward the dogwood trees.

Past the trees, they walked up a little hill. Dan got there first and shaded his eyes with his hand. He looked out over the prairie.

"Is that them?" Annie Mae asked.

She pointed.

"I think that's their wagon. But I don't see them."

Annie Mae felt twinge of fear. Where were they? Was someone arguing with Uncle Michael about the claim?

"They must be on the other side of the wagon," Dan said.

Annie Mae started walking more quickly.

"I wonder what's down there," Dan said. He pointed

to the rocky valley between them and the wagon in the distance.

"Rocks," Annie Mae said. "We can look at them on our way."

They scrambled down into the little valley. Long grass and trees grew all along the sides. It was shadier in the valley, and quieter. Annie Mae was surprised how much cooler it felt.

"Hey, look," Dan said. Up ahead of them was a ring of rocks. A campfire still smoldered in it.

"Moonlighters," Annie Mae said. "I hope they get caught."

"Listen!" Dan said.

Annie Mae listened. "I hear water dripping."

They followed the sound to a rock outcropping. Water was seeping down onto another rock. It formed a little pool.

"Hurray!" Dan said.

"We'll have good water close by, until Pa can dig us a well," Annie Mae said.

"What did you find?" a familiar voice called. It was Libby!

Annie Mae ran to hug her.

"Did you get the next claim?" she asked.

"Of course," Libby said. "You don't think my pa would let anyone else have it, do you?"

Annie Mae laughed. Uncle Michael would be just the one to start an argument over a claim.

"We found a spring," Dan said. "It's close to both our claims."

Libby followed them to the rock pool. She cupped her hand for a cool drink.

"I'm going to go tell Pa," Dan said.

"Want to come?" Annie Mae asked Libby.

"No, I have to help Ma," she said. "I was supposed to tell you all to come for dinner as soon as your tent is pitched. Ma's already making biscuits."

Dan rubbed his stomach.

"Come on, Annie Mae. Let's hurry and get Pa."

Annie Mae waved to her cousin and then followed Dan back to the wagon. Pa had put up the tent. He was taking supplies out of the wagon.

"Pa!" Dan called. "We found water."

"Uncle Michael and Aunt Ellen got the next claim over. They want us to come for dinner," Annie Mae said.

Pa laughed. "You two are full of good news."

"Looks like moonlighters have been in that valley, too." Annie Mae scowled. "The cheaters."

Pa grabbed another crate from the back of the wagon and set it on the ground. As he did, Annie Mae saw him looking toward the trees. She looked, too.

Three men were coming toward them. Two were leading their horses. And each man had his hand on a gun in his holster.

Claim Jumpers

"Who are they?" Dan asked.

"They want our land," Annie Mae said.

"You don't know that for sure," Dan argued.

Annie Mae was sure. She hadn't forgotten the preacher's words. What else could they be doing?

"Get in the tent," Pa said.

Pa's tone scared Annie Mae. She and Dan ran quickly into the tent. They peeked through the flaps. The man in the middle walked up to Pa and tipped his hat.

"You and your young ones are on my claim," he said.

Annie Mae felt her face get hot. How dare he say this was his claim?

"No," Pa said in a steady voice. "You and your men are on *my* claim."

"We've been here a long time," the man said. "But we're reasonable. We know you need a home for your family. We'd be willing to give the claim over to you for $25."

Annie Mae felt as though she was boiling. She was really angry. But she was also scared. Pa's Winchester rifle lay on the ground outside. As she watched, one of the men picked it up and held it loosely in one arm.

"They must be the moonlighters who set up camp in the valley," she whispered.

"Maybe they're outlaws," Dan whispered back. His eyes were wide. He looked scared, too. "You don't think they'll hurt Pa, do you?"

"I'm not going to wait to find out," she said. "I'm going to get Uncle Michael."

"I'm coming, too," Dan said.

He followed her as she climbed over crates, Ma's dresser, and an old trunk. They slid carefully under the back of the tent. She could still hear the man talking to Pa, but not what he was saying.

Annie Mae and Dan walked in a straight line away from the tent. It hid them from view for a while. Then they started running.

"Hey!" a man's voice shouted. "Come back here!"

Annie Mae didn't look back. She grabbed Dan's hand and kept running. She ran up over the rise. They scrambled down one side of the little valley and up the other. Soon they could see Libby helping Aunt Ellen put up their tent. Uncle Michael was saddling one of the horses.

"Help!" Annie Mae gasped as she got closer. Libby dropped the wooden tent stake she was holding. She ran to Annie Mae.

"Three men," Annie Mae said breathlessly. "On our claim. They want $25 or . . ." her voice trailed off. She didn't know what they would do if Pa didn't give them the money.

"Libby, ride that way," Uncle Michael said pointing. "See if you can catch up with those two soldiers who just rode by. Hurry!"

Libby mounted the horse that Uncle Michael had finished saddling. She kicked the horse hard in the ribs and galloped off.

Uncle Michael picked up his rifle from the wagon seat where it had been lying.

"The preacher yesterday said to settle arguments in the land office," Annie Mae said.

"I don't suppose those claim jumpers on your land heard that sermon," Uncle Michael said. He didn't look at her.

"I'm coming with you," Aunt Ellen said. She

brought out a revolver from a wooden trunk.

"You two stay put," Uncle Michael said.

Annie Mae pressed her lips together to keep from saying "no." Dan slipped his hand into hers as they watched their aunt and uncle hurry off. Soon they were down in the valley and Annie Mae couldn't see them anymore.

"Come on," she said. She pulled Dan behind her.

"You're going to get us in trouble," Dan said.

"We won't go all the way," Annie Mae said. "We can watch from the trees. They might need our help."

"How can we help?" he asked.

"I don't know," Annie Mae said. "Pick up some rocks to throw. We can't just stay put and do nothing."

Annie Mae and Dan reached the cover of the dogwood trees in time to see Uncle Michael and Aunt Ellen striding toward Pa. Pa was sitting down on a crate. One of the men was taking the tent down. The other two were loading boxes back into the wagon.

Annie Mae saw red. How dare those men touch Ma's things? How dare they try to take her family's claim—their new life? Hadn't they gone through a lifetime of trouble just to get here? Two years of waiting, mud, rivers, and almost losing their wagon. And, worst of all, losing Ma.

The men saw Aunt Ellen and Uncle Michael. They turned to face them. Annie Mae held her breath.

Suddenly she heard horses' hooves galloping near.

Two soldiers riding sleek, black horses were riding with Libby.

The men saw the soldiers and ran to their horses. They jumped on them and galloped off. One soldier galloped after them. Another stopped to talk to Pa.

"My orders are to ride around and see to it there's no trouble," he said. "If you have any more trouble, I want to hear about it."

Pa nodded. Annie Mae and Dan ran to Pa and hugged him. He put an arm around each of them.

Libby got down and stood between her parents.

"I thought I'd never find those soldiers. It seemed like that ride took forever," she said.

"You were hardly gone any time at all," Aunt Ellen said. "I sure was worried about you when I saw you riding over the hill, though. I didn't know what those men would do."

"I thought I told you two to stay put," Uncle Michael said. He frowned at Annie Mae and Dan. Annie Mae looked down at the ground. Why did he decide to look at her now?

"I was afraid," Annie Mae said. "I thought you might need help."

Uncle Michael let out a sigh. Pa shook his head.

"Disobeying your uncle," Pa said. "What would Ma say about you two?"

Annie Mae felt a knot growing in her throat.

"Annie Mae made me come with her!" Dan yelled.

Uncle Michael laughed.

"I remember using that excuse a time or two, Danny boy," he said. "It's time to stop letting your bossy big sister tell you what to do."

Annie Mae smiled. Uncle Michael was almost teasing her again, wasn't he?

"The claim jumpers are gone, and that's the important thing," Aunt Ellen said.

Everyone nodded. Annie Mae looked in the direction the soldiers had chased the men. She wondered if the claim jumpers would come back.

Filing the Claim

"I still think you should have let me stay," Annie Mae said. She and Dan were riding Blue. Pa was riding Belle. Up ahead, Uncle Michael rode one horse and Aunt Ellen and Libby rode another. They were all on their way to Guthrie to file their claims.

Pa sighed.

"We both should have stayed," Dan said. "With the Winchester."

"I don't want to argue anymore," Pa said.

"Uncle Michael is taking Aunt Ellen and Libby

with him. I"m not going to leave you two alone, either."

"What if those claim jumpers try to take our land again?" Annie Mae asked.

"Or steal our things?" Dan added.

"Ma's things," Annie Mae said.

"We will cross those bridges when we come to them," Pa said.

"No more bridges. Please," Dan said. He giggled.

Annie Mae had to laugh, too. Even Pa smiled. She knew Pa was just as worried about the claim jumpers as they were.

They rode the rest of the way to Guthrie in silence. Along the way, they saw tents, horses, cows, and people. A few of the settlers were even starting to build log houses.

It wasn't hard to find Guthrie. They knew they were there when they saw all the people and heard all the noise. There was a line of people in front of an unpainted wooden building—the land office. The line stretched so far Annie Mae could barely see where it ended.

"We'll never get to the front of that line," Annie Mae said. To herself she added, And there might be people ahead of us who claim our land. Our new home.

"Don't worry," Pa said. "We'll get to the front of the line eventually. Maybe in a few days."

Uncle Michael chuckled and nodded.

"At least we're finally here," Aunt Ellen said.

They found a place to tie the horses in front of the train station down the hill. Then they got into line.

All around them was the noise of a town being built. Men yelled and argued with one another about where the streets should be. Hammers and saws sang up and down the streets as stores were built. Wagons with supplies seemed to be going in a hurry in all directions.

The people in line were mostly men with their jackets off and hats pushed back. They carried bedrolls and carpetbags with their few belongings. Some of them even had cooking pots and pans with them.

"Do we have to cook dinner in line?" Dan asked.

"Probably," Annie Mae said.

"We didn't bring any pots," Libby said.

"You three can look around," Pa said. "We'll wait here."

"Go on," Aunt Ellen said. She pushed Libby, who was hanging back—trying to be one of the grown-ups, Annie Mae thought.

"Go have a good look at the new town," Uncle Michael said. "They say Guthrie is going to be the most important town in the territory."

"We'll come back and tell you all about it," Annie Mae said. She grabbed her cousin with one hand and Dan with the other. She pulled them after her.

44

"We'll still be here when you get back," Pa called after her.

Annie Mae led the way to the bottom of the hill and the train station. Right next to Guthrie Station there were at least 50 white tents—the Santa Fe House hotel. They walked by one of the big dining tents. Annie Mae could smell beef stew and cornbread. Her mouth watered. Libby closed her eyes and breathed deeply.

"I don't suppose anyone has money for eating in there," Libby said.

"Maybe we can get filled up if we just take a deep breath," Annie Mae said.

"Seems like we almost could," Dan said.

They walked down to the Cottonwood River. The water was low against the banks and muddy brown. A man was standing under a tree with a little table. A group of people stood around him.

"They're gambling," Libby whispered.

"I'm going to watch," Annie Mae said out loud. She moved closer. Dan and Libby stayed behind her.

"Watch closely, as I, Harry Travers, fastest man alive, move the shells around," he said. Annie Mae giggled. She watched as he moved three walnut shells around on the table. Another man put a nickel down on the table.

"Now guess which shell hides the pea," Harry said. The man pointed to the one in the middle. Harry

lifted it. Nothing was under it. The man shook his head. Harry put the nickel in his pocket.

"Ah, little lady," Harry said to Annie Mae. "I'll give you one free guess where the pea is. Watch closely." Harry showed her which shell he put the pea under. Then he began moving them around with both hands—in and around one another. Annie Mae watched closely. When he stopped, she pointed to the one on the left. The pea was under it! How Annie wished she had a nickel to bet!

A man behind her slapped a nickel on the table.

"This is easy," he said.

Harry moved the shells around again. Only this time his hands went faster. Annie Mae got dizzy trying

to keep up. When he finally stopped, she wasn't sure where the pea was.

The man pointed to the one on the left. The pea wasn't there.

"Huh! There isn't a pea under any of them," he said.

Harry lifted the shell from the one in the middle. The pea was under it. The people standing around laughed.

"He tricked you good," one said.

Annie Mae heard the train coming. She hurried the others back to Guthrie Station. She wanted to see who would get off. They got back just as the train pulled in. Before it had fully stopped, people were jumping off and running to find claims in town.

"I don't know why they're hurrying," Annie Mae said. "I bet that there isn't even one town lot left to claim."

"Maybe there are some lots we haven't seen," Libby said.

"Look!" Dan said suddenly. They all stared.

"Those are the soldiers I went to get," Libby said.

The two men were walking toward the train station. They both looked dusty and tired.

The soldiers saw Libby and smiled.

"We're still looking for those claim jumpers," the one with brown hair said. "But we'll catch them."

"And then we'll send them back to Kansas," the other added. "We don't want people like that in the territory."

"What about all the moonlighters?" Annie Mae asked.

"We'll run any of them off that we find, too."

"Good," Libby said angrily. "Moonlighters are nothing but cheats."

Annie Mae and Dan laughed.

"You're starting to sound like some other people I know," Dan said.

"I don't know what you mean," Annie Mae added, teasing.

"Let us know if you see those men around town," the soldier with brown hair said.

Dan saluted. The soldiers grinned and saluted back.

Annie Mae and the others ran up the hill to the claim-filing line. It didn't take long to find Pa, Uncle Michael, and Aunt Ellen. They hadn't moved very far. Annie Mae thought it must be the slowest line on earth. It was worse than waiting for your birthday or Christmas.

All day, Annie Mae and Libby and Dan explored Guthrie. Tents had been put up on building lots all over town. One tent was a general store. Another tent was a post office. One tent was even a bank! Annie Mae wondered how they kept the money safe.

They watched the building and the arguing and the laughing. Most of the people seemed as happy as Annie Mae that they were about to start a new life in a new place.

The sun was sinking lower in the sky. Finally, Pa and Uncle Michael and Aunt Ellen were near the door of the land office.

Annie Mae couldn't believe it was really about to happen.

"Can we watch you file?" Annie Mae asked Pa.

"Of course," Pa said. "We'll be next."

Annie Mae stood silently with her cousin and brother. She looked up at Uncle Michael. His eyes were shining, and he was smiling. She could tell he was very happy.

Annie Mae didn't have to wonder what Ma would have looked like right then. She would have looked the same. Uncle Michael looked down at her and smiled. She smiled back.

Soon they were standing before the man with the big land book. He handed Pa a piece of paper to fill out. There was a place for his name and the date.

Annie Mae watched as Pa wrote *Albert Durkee* in his best handwriting. Then he wrote the date—*April 23, 1889.*

He told the man seated at the table that he claimed the Northeast Quarter of Section 25. The man turned the pages of the land book. He finally stopped and ran his finger down the left-hand side of the page.

Annie Mae held her breath. What if someone else's name was already entered there? What if—

"Section 25?" the man asked. "Northeast Quarter?"

"That's right," Pa said.

The man took Pa's piece of paper.

"Albert Durkee," the man said. He wrote it in the big book. "That will be $14 for the filing fee."

Pa counted out the money slowly. Annie Mae let out the breath she was holding. She didn't think she would ever feel this happy again. The claim was really, truly theirs now. This was, finally, the beginning of their new life.

ABOUT THIS BOOK

In the 1800s Oklahoma was occupied by various Indian tribes. Sometime in the 1870s, Colonel Elias Boudinot, a Cherokee lawyer, pointed out something interesting. Two million acres in Oklahoma had not been assigned to any tribe. This area of land became known as the Unassigned Lands or the Oklahoma Territory.

The first reaction of some people was to enter the land and begin homesteading. David L. Payne, a Kansas politician, was one of the first to lead a group of people into this land. It was not legal. Before the territory could be settled, the government had to open it officially for that purpose.

Payne and his followers were turned back by United States troops and Indian Bureau officials. They began promoting the opening of this land. They lobbied in Washington, D.C., and wrote letters to newspapers around the country. Their effort became known as the Boomer movement.

In January 1889, a bill was introduced in Congress that would allow the president to open the Oklahoma Territory to settlers. On March 2, 1889, President Grover Cleveland signed the bill into law. President Henry Harrison took office on March 4, 1889. He decided to open the land by holding a "land run." (Four more areas of Oklahoma were opened to land runs in later years. But this one was the first.)

For the people who had been waiting, like Annie Mae's family, it was a happy day when they got the news. Some people were so worried about there not being enough land to go around that they crossed the line ahead of time. At first, these people were called moonlighters. During the court contests that followed, the moonlighters became known as *sooners*—because they went over sooner than the rest. Many of them lost their claims.

The mad dash for land in Oklahoma Territory on April 22, 1889, lasted only a day. Many people, however, had waited near the border for years. After the run, there was still some waiting left to do. Homesteaders had to live on their land for five years. During that time, they had to make improvements, such as planting crops and building a house or barn. Then, at the end of five years, they would finally get the deed to their land.

Many people thought that the word Oklahoma meant "beautiful land." It is really made up from the Choctaw words meaning "Land of the Red People." But for people like Annie Mae and her family, Oklahoma truly was a beautiful land.